M000218396

Being
Zen

This book belongs to

_____

© 2001 Modus Vivendi Publishing Inc.
All rights reserved.

Published by:
Modus Vivendi Publishing Inc.
3859 Laurentian Autoroute
Laval, Quebec
Canada H7L 3H7

Cover and inside page design: Marc Alain
Translation by: Scott & Aronoff

Picture Credits: © SuperStock and Eyewire

Legal Deposit: 1st Quarter 2001
National Library of Canada

Canadian Cataloguing in Publication Data
Desbois, Hervé
    The way of Zen
    (Heartfelt Series)
    Translation of: Être Zen
    ISBN: 2-89523-055-2
    1. Zen Buddhism. 2. Zen Buddhism - Pictorial works.
    I. Title. II. Series.
BQ9265.6.D4713 2001   294.3'927   C00-942054-1

Canada We acknowledge the financial support of the Government
of Canada through the Book Publishing Industry Development
Program (BPIDP) for our publishing activities.

Being
Zen

HERVÉ DESBOIS

MV PUBLISHING

"He who is Master of himself is greater than he who is Master of the world."

Buddha

Zen, with its tradition of secular teachings and practices, is like a corner of nature that has not been touched by the human hand. Nature where calm, serenity and harmony prevail. Nature whose purity has the transparency of cold spring water.

Whatever the vehicle chosen, the path of wisdom can be long and tortuous. But the spirit that attains higher states of light is like a mirror that reflects everything perfectly.

Like any philosophical or religious path, Zen is above all an adventure, one that involves inner work. But the spirit of Zen is also projected outwardly, as if the two aspects are inseparable. The environment based on Zen contributes to the peace of the spirit, but is also the reflection of that peace. Purity of line, fluidity of form, simplicity of arrangement: Zen space pays homage to nature, beauty and perfection.

"Each moment eclipses the moment before. Whatever happens, this is the present. Make your house here."

Zen Meditation

Deep Within

I seek peace,
Buffeted by the storm
Of an unsettled life.
Where is the truth?

In this troubled world
I feel fragile,
Like a twig
Bent by the wind.

Am I cause
Or effect?
Am I only a reflection,
A mere thing?

A drop of water
Drunk by the earth?
A poor stone
Thrown into the water?

Yet I see
What lies dormant,
What I keep inside,
Deep within me.

So much beauty
Is wrapped in silence,
So much power
To be released.

> "Remaining angry is like grasping a burning coal to throw it at somebody. You are the one who is burned."

Buddha

"I'll never forgive him!"
This is what an angry man said to an old sage who lived, alone and secluded, on a very small island south of the big island of Kyushu, in the Japanese archipelago.
The old sage looked at the angry man, his face impassive. But his clear eyes showed great kindness. This man was known and venerated throughout the islands, and people came from as far away as the port of Kita, far north of Kyushu, to ask him for advice. Sometimes, people involved in disagreements even came to present their grievances together so that the old man could decide in favour of one or other -- or both, as sometimes occurred.
Oda was intimidated and did not know how to react to the sage's silence. It was anger that had brought him to the humble dwelling of the old man. However, the more he spoke, the more he felt his anger wane. So he continued speaking, explaining in great detail everything his neighbour had done to him and had refused him, without neglecting to mention how good and generous he, Oda, had been in the past towards this selfish and dishonest neighbour.
"You understand, Master, for me, this is a debt of honour rather than a matter of all the little services he has refused me."

(...)

But the old sage continue to gaze intently at Oda without saying a word. Since he did not answer, and did not ask any questions, Oda searched further back in his memory to find other torments his neighbour might have inflicted on him. He thought in this way he would rekindle the anger and resentment in his heart, which he felt steadily abating. But the more he searched, the more he discovered things that he himself had done to harm others. Oda stopped speaking and lowered his eyes. The old man, who had still not budged, put his hand on Oda's shoulder and smiled kindly at him.

"Who is wrong, who is right? You came to ask questions for which you already had the answers. By sifting the sand of the river, the gold prospector finds the nugget. You have found the gold of truth."

Then the old sage gestured that the conversation was over. When Oda turned to go back to his village, the old sage called to him one last time.

"Never forget that the wind of anger brings only clouds and thunder. Do not let yourself be carried away by the storm."

"If hatred answers hatred, how will hatred end?"

Buddha

> "The garden
> Promise of the infinite virtue of nature
> Close at hand."

Haiku (short Japanese poem)

Zen cuisine is simple, colourful, and based on fresh, quality ingredients: vegetables, usually raw or lightly cooked, fish, rice, soba (buckwheat noodles), udon (wheat noodles), etc.

The Zen kitchen has a spiritual dimension, since it has to provide "fertile ground" for the life of the spirit. Moreover, the aesthetics of the presentation of a meal are as important as the quality of the ingredients.

And what could be more refreshing than a crisp salad? Quick and easy to make, salads offer infinite possibilities for variation.

The salad dressing helps provide that desirable touch of originality. Here is a very simple little oriental salad that may be accompanied by one of the two dressings presented below.

Oriental Salad
- Cooked chicken (this may be leftovers)
- Bean sprouts
- 2 cucumbers
- 1 or 2 carrots

(...)

Prepare the bean sprouts by cutting off both ends.
Peel the cucumbers, cut them in half lengthwise,
remove the seeds with a spoon, then cut each half
into thin strips about ten centimetres long.
Peel the carrots and cut them into thin strips.
Do the same with the cooked chicken.
Arrange all the ingredients attractively and add the
salad dressing of your choice.
One final little touch typical of Zen philosophy:
add a few edible flowers.

Japanese-style Vinaigrette
Combine:
- 1 tablespoon rice vinegar
- 2 tablespoons vegetable oil
- 1 teaspoon soy sauce
- Salt and pepper

Ginger Vinaigrette
Combine:
- 1 tablespoon rice vinegar
- 1 tablespoon vegetable oil
- 1 tablespoon sesame oil
- 1 tablespoon grated fresh ginger root
- 1 teaspoon soy sauce

"Life is not a problem to be solved,
but a reality to be experienced."

Buddha

"When you see a wise man, think of matching
him in virtue. When you see a man
who is without wisdom, examine yourself."

Confucius

"We sometimes forget the pain we suffer,
never the pain we cause."

Avâdanas

"The path of duty is always close,
but man seeks it far away."

Chinese proverb

"The grass of the fields
Under my soles
Releases its fragrance."

Haiku by Shiki Masaoka

"He who has put aside envy, hatred and
foolishness is like a polished mirror."

Buddha

Slides

The white lily
Lives each moment
Without movement.

Cherry blossoms
White virginities
Fragrance of freedom.

Snowflakes
Dizzying carousel
Of snow stars.

Bird song
Soars high
Call without words.

Song of water
In the reeds
Music of rest.

Festive nature
Gives itself each day
To the heart at peace.

> "Joy is everything; one must know
> how to extract it."
>
> Confucius

It was one of those October days I love -- fiery nature against the backdrop of a blue sky. The weather was mild but not hot. Through the half-open window of my office, I absentmindedly contemplated the spectacle. And suddenly I had enough of being shut up inside, sitting in front of my computer, waiting for inspiration that didn't come. I soon found some errands to run to justify going out. Going for a walk, I should say! But it's true that I was out of bread and the bulb of my reading lamp was burned out. I put on my coat and dashed out. Ah! the air was so fresh and the smell of the air so pleasant -- not yet the powerful odours of autumn, but no longer the fragrance of summer. That day nature seemed to be flirting with time, slipping back and forth between two seasons -- one last escapade before the great leap into winter.

"My goodness, it's Indian summer!"

The village, too, seemed to be in the midst of a truce, bathed in ephemeral tranquillity. As I crossed the bridge over the river, I was in ecstasy at the beauty of the multicoloured foliage mirrored in the perfectly calm water. Some trees still wore their green garb, while others already looked like blazing torches, in shades of fiery reds and yellows.

(...)

After several detours to drink in all these splendours, I returned home with the bread and the light bulb. After putting away my purchases, I realized that the only money I had left was some small change, but I was sure that I had left with a few bills in my pocket. I searched in vain in coat and pants, turning out all the pockets and checking for holes in the linings, but my money had vanished! My walk must have filled me with serenity because, strangely enough, I did not feel the least bit annoyed.

In the evening, I told this story to my wife, who had just told me what an awful day she'd had. She seemed more upset than I was by the loss.

"How much?"

"Oh I don't know. Maybe forty dollars."

"Forty dollars! That's quite a bit of money. For me, that's two hours of work, you know."

In a sense, she was right. Every penny is important and valuable, especially if it is well earned! And it is always stupid to lose money. But I couldn't help smiling.

"Doesn't it bother you?"

"No, as a matter of fact. I just hope that whoever found it really needs it."

> "Wisdom is not meditation on death,
> but on life."
>
> Spinoza

"If a person speaks or acts with a pure mind,
then happiness follows, like the shadow
that never leaves him."

Buddha

KARMA: (Sanskrit word meaning "action" or
"work") a basic concept in Hinduism, Buddhism
and Jainism. The doctrine of karma states that
one's state in this life is a result of actions (both
physical and mental) in past incarnations, and that
actions in this life can determine one's destiny in
future incarnations. *(The Columbia Encyclopedia)*
Karma is a fundamental principle, a spiritual law
that may be summed up as follows: "We reap what
we sow."
Stated in this way, karma seems to be a universal
law. St. Paul's Epistle to the Galatians in a way
explains the very essence of karma.
However, the law of karma has a special meaning.
According to this principle, there are no punish-
ments, only consequences. Therefore, it is not God
that is responsible for the pleasures or pains we
experience. Every human being, despite appear-
ances, is responsible for his or her situation.

(...)

But what about people who never seem to have any problems in spite of all the evil they do? The law of karma says that the consequences of our acts do not necessarily materialize in this life. If we suffer today, it is perhaps because of our karma from a former life. And, conversely, we will be able to benefit in a future life from the karma we create today.

Confucius said, "Act towards others as you would want them to act towards you." This golden rule, which certainly contributes to good karma, should, however, apply to groups as well as individuals. Because karma also concerns families, communities, nations, and even the human race. As individuals, we can therefore benefit from, or suffer from, the consequences of collective actions.

For each cause, there is an effect.

For each effect, there is a cause.

"With our thoughts, we create the world."

Buddha

"The faults of others are easy to see;
our own are hard to see."

Buddha

"The truths we least like to learn
are the ones we most need to know."

Chinese proverb

"On waking, I learn anew the dance
of the flowering cherry tree
The endless work of the mirror
The sensation of sunlight."

Haiku

"It is not weeds that choke out the grain,
it is the negligence of the farmer."

Confucius

"Water does not stay on the mountains,
nor revenge on a great heart."

Chinese proverb

"A good action is one that causes no regrets and
whose fruit is gathered with joy and serenity."

Buddha

Signs of Time

We look to the sky
Without understanding the messages,
What the sun says,
What the clouds tell of,
If the words were known.
It was a long time ago
And memories have lost
All track of time.

We hear the wind clearly
But without grasping anything more,
Without really listening
To what its language whispers.
If the path was traced,
Who sees it now?
The signs have vanished
From the gaze of a new faith.

If time carries the signs
Of all the things that pass,
Why does history always get stuck
In the same ruts?

Beyond the lie
The truth is hidden.
Its roots burrow deep
Into the heart of simplicity

Each one must find it.

"Summer wind
Sheets of white paper on the table
Snatched away."

Haiku by Shiki Masaoka

The door was open, letting the sweet smells of summer into the quiet house. Tentatively, I stepped inside. Everything was quiet, as if asleep in the torpor of the afternoon.
"Hello! Is anyone here?"
Movement upstairs.
"Vincent? Are you there?"
"Harold? Come in, come in and make yourself at home. I'll be down in a minute."
I looked around for the old familiar couch. But I was surprised to discover an unfamiliar house, with no resemblance at all to what it had been before. The last time I had been here was a year ago. Vincent had organized a small reception to celebrate his departure for Japan. I remembered the odds and ends that had furnished the place, such a mix of styles that no single style really stood out. What met my eyes now was a spare decor, reduced to essentials. The furniture, all made of natural materials, was simple, but refined and elegant. Turning around, I surveyed the living room, the kitchen and the dining room; the ground floor was just one big open space. The arrangement and colours induced calm.

(...)

I decided to sit down in an armchair with a pale bamboo frame. Its cushions of coarsely woven linen welcomed me into their softness. On a small low table, magazines and books on the Buddha, Zen and Japanese cuisine were scattered in carefully calculated disorder. Intrigued, I flipped through them. I suddenly recalled a letter that Vincent had written to me from a Buddhist monastery where he had stayed for a while, in which he had written "the outside is the reflection of the inside."

I looked again at the decor of the house, and I couldn't help imagining the changes my friend must have gone through. How would he look? Head shaven, dressed like a Tibetan monk, palms together, chanting prayers in an incomprehensible mumble? I'm ashamed to admit it, but at that exact moment I thought of leaving, I was so afraid I would no longer recognize Vincent. But we were friends, after all, and I regained my composure, prepared to face any eventuality. Just then, I heard his footsteps on the stairs.

And Vincent appeared, his arms open, already hugging me warmly. He stepped back, looked at me for a moment, then burst out laughing. He must have sensed my discomfort.

"Hey, you look like you've seen a ghost!"

A ghost, yes, but with the same faded jeans and white tee-shirt, his hair as black and abundant as before. And I couldn't think of anything to say to him but the old platitude, "You haven't changed a bit!"

> **"It is hard to catch a black cat in a dark room, especially when it is not there."**
>
> Chinese proverb

"Sand between my fingers
The clouds disperse
Morning autumn."

Haiku by Shiki Masaoka

An island of stone in a sea of white sand, a river of gravel streaked with straight or curving waves -- karesansui, or dry gardens, are an important art form in Zen philosophy. Natural harmony, calm, and subtle beauty, everything in the inorganic garden is conducive to contemplation and meditation, providing a path to serenity by abolishing worldly concerns.

The rock partly submerged in sand and the gravel that surrounds it are typical of Zen gardens, which are rich in symbols despite their apparent austerity. They create a spirit of serenity, serenity without which the spirit cannot find peace.

The contrast between the immobility of the stone and the fluidity of the lines traced in the sand or gravel represents a concept that is important in Zen, and that has many interpretations. One of these is that the spirit seeking serenity must still live amidst the currents of a constantly changing world, a world that never stops moving around us. Like a Zen garden, a meal should be an island of tranquillity, a symbol of relaxation but also of pleasure, like an oasis in the frenzy of our busy Western days.

Chicken Teriyaki

- Chicken breasts
- 2 tablespoons sake (rice wine)
- 4 tablespoons soy sauce
- 4 tablespoons mirin (sweet rice wine)
- 2 tablespoons sugar

Cut up the chicken breasts into large pieces.
Mix the sake, soy sauce, mirin, and sugar. Marinate the chicken pieces in this preparation in the refrigerator for at least 30 minutes, or longer if you want a stronger flavour.
Heat a little vegetable oil in a frying pan and cook the chicken pieces on both sides over a low fire.
Add the marinade and simmer over a low fire until the sauce thickens.
Serve garnished with finely chopped fresh shallots and a little grated ginger. Add colour and nutrition with a selection of steamed vegetables.

"The world is blind. Rare are those who see."

Buddha

"Excess kills more surely than swords."

Chinese proverb

"To move a mountain,
start by taking away small stones."

Confucius

"Life is like a story. What is important is not
how long it is, but how good it is."

Seneca

"Chattering is scum on water,
action is a drop of gold."

Chinese proverb

"Better than a thousand meaningless words is
a single sensible word, which can bring
calm to the one who listens to it."

Buddha

The Quest

Through the ages
Lessons, always the same,
Revealed by the sages
Illuminate human paths.

Taught, seldom learned,
Knowledge dies,
Ignored in the contempt
Of the man who will not see.

Voice of heaven,
Heavenly path,
A road takes us
Out of earthly chaos.

To be bodhi
As the Buddha was,
Man waits for the Messiah,
The Saviour, the Maitreya.

Wisdom,
The quest is immortal.
Let us not cease
To seek your wings.

"The knowledge that is not supplemented
daily decreases every day."

Chinese proverb

"Do not be afraid of being slow,
only of stopping."

Confucius

"The person who, after having been careless,
becomes attentive, illuminates the earth like
the moon emerging from the clouds."

Buddha

"Sick in bed
Through the bamboo screen
The autumn butterfly comes to visit."

Haiku by Soseki Natsume

"The superior man asks nothing except
from himself. The vulgar,
worthless man asks everything of others."

Confucius

"With time and patience,
the leaf of the mulberry tree becomes silk."

Chinese proverb